Weird, Wondrous & Historic Pubs of the United Kingdom

Mikey G. Swann

Step inside and lay thine eyes upon,

History in all its glory,

Forever remembered,

Forever living on

ACKNOWLEDGEMENTS

The completion of this book could not have been made possible without the help of others. Their support and contribution is sincerely appreciated and gratefully acknowledged.

I would like to extend my thanks to the following people;

- My mam Michelle and friend Sarah for proofreading

- Tom Mellor for the foreword

- Annie Spratt for giving permission to use her image on the back cover

- And finally, a special thanks to all the pub staff, including; managers, breweries and retailers for kindly providing information for inclusion in this book

The information in this book is true and complete to the best of my knowledge and was correct at the time of going to press. All photographs included in this book are the property of the author and publisher except where stated and are protected in U.K. law by the Copyright, Designs and Patents Act 1988. Personal information in photographs that are visible such as; faces and car registrations have been concealed for privacy reasons. Permissions have been sought and accepted by all public houses featured. The author and publisher disclaim any liability in connection with the use of this information.

ISBN: 9781089962793

FOREWORD

As brewers, pubs are our bread and butter; likewise the communities that they serve. And just as every community has its quirks and own characteristics, so do the pubs! The expression "wouldn't it be boring if we were all the same" is very apt here. What makes Britain's culture of public houses so unique is the individuality of those public houses and it's wonderful to have a book that celebrates this. Everyone likes a story and a snippet of information which they can pass on to their friends and the varied examples here are a great excuse to call in and sample the atmosphere that our pub heritage has in abundance. Should be kept in the car for reference!

Tom Mellor – Co-founder of Wold Top Brewery and Spirit of Yorkshire Distillery

INTRODUCTION

Welcome to the United Kingdom; the home of cricket, fish & chips and James Bond. We are also home to some of the weirdest, wonderful and most historic pubs in the world and you now have the chance to see some of these for yourself in my book; Weird, Wondrous & Historic Pubs of the United Kingdom.

Throughout life, we set ourselves goals that are based on our passions; passions that get us up in the morning and motivate us to complete them. My passion has been to seek out the pubs of this great nation and to find out what makes them stand out from the rest. I want to fly the flag for our country's drinking establishments and give them the recognition they deserve.

My adventure has taken me to some places I never knew existed and this is what has made this journey so remarkable. Each drinkery that has made it into this book has given me a unique experience to take away, and I am now honoured to be sharing these discoveries with you. This book will allow you to step into the past of these weird and wondrous pubs, and read about the historic stories they carry.

So please join me on my quest around the United Kingdom.

Happy reading!

Mikey

CONTENTS

CAMBRIDGESHIRE

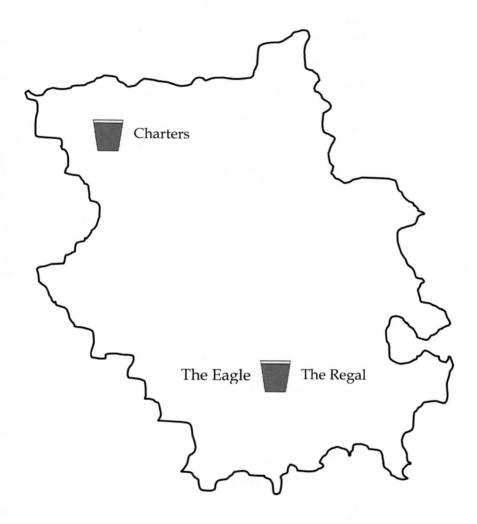

Charters

The Eagle   The Regal

"The problem with the world is that everyone is a few drinks behind."

– Humphrey Bogart

Charters Bar
Town Bridge, Peterborough, PE1 1FP
01733 315700
www.charters-bar.com

Built in 1907, this 176ft 'Leendert-R' continental barge originally worked on the canals of Holland, Belgium and Germany up until 1990, carrying cargo such as sand and grain. It was brought across to the UK and converted into a bar and restaurant in 1991 and is reputedly the largest converted pub barge in the country.

The Regal
38-39 St. Andrew's Street, Cambridge, CB2 3AR
01223 366459

When this pub re-opened in 2000, it became the largest public house in the country. Built in 1937 as the Regal Cinema, it claimed to be the latest and most up-to-date cinema in Cambridge. It eventually closed 60 years later in 1997 where it stood empty until it was re-opened by the JD Wetherspoon company.

The Eagle
8 Bene't Street, Cambridge, CB2 3QN
01223 505020

This pub dates back to the 14th century and is full of fascinating features; namely in the so-called 'RAF Bar' where the ceiling is covered in graffiti made by RAF servicemen during World War II, using candle flames. The pub became famous though on February 28th 1953 when Francis Crick and James Watson made a public announcement to the whole pub that they had discovered "the secret of life"; the discovery of DNA.

DERBYSHIRE

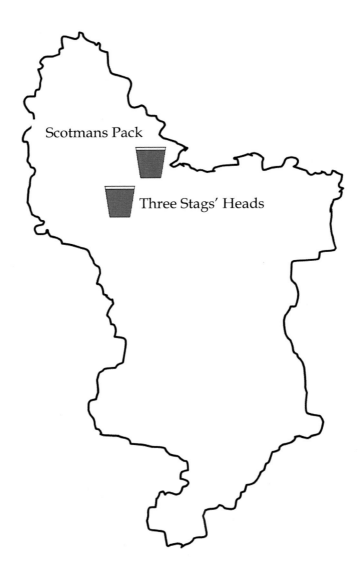

Scotmans Pack

Three Stags' Heads

"The first draught serveth for health, the second for pleasure, the third for shame, the fourth for madness."

– Sir Walter Raleigh

Three Stags' Heads
Mires Lane, Wardlow, SK17 8RW
01298 872268

Located around 11 miles from Buxton on the A623, this quaint country pub is definitely different from most. It boasts old photographs and flagstone floors, not to mention a warm open fire upon arrival, but behind these pleasant features lays a sinister story. Years previously when the pub was having major alterations, a mummified cat was found. It was alleged to have been buried alive as it was believed, at the time, to ward off evil spirits.

Scotsmans Pack
School Lane, Hathersage, S32 1BZ
01433 650253
www.scotsmanspackcountryinn.co.uk

More than 200 years ago, the area would get regular visits by 'packmen' who would offer goods and services to townsfolk. The name of this pub takes its name from Scottish packmen, who would sell their fabric to farmers across the county and would stay for the night on their way to Sheffield to rest their horses. Within this pub is Little John's giant chair, the friend and fellow outlaw of Robin Hood. If that wasn't enough, one can take a short stroll up the road to see Little John's grave in St Michael's Church. As you can see below, his name is not to be taken literally...

Did you know...

This chair was won in a wager by Major G. Lucas of the Manchester Regiment from Lieutenant A. Sunderland M.C., Royal Tank Regiment in 1950.

GREATER LONDON &
CITY OF LONDON

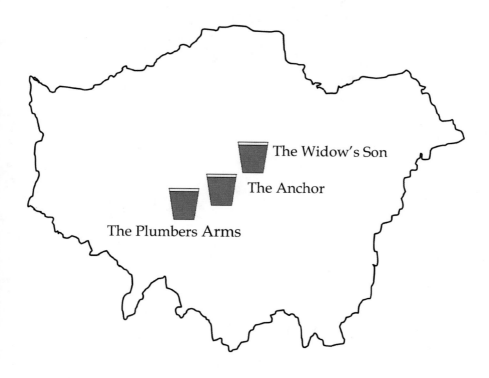

The Widow's Son

The Anchor

The Plumbers Arms

"Always carry a flagon of whisky in case of snakebite and
furthermore always carry a small snake."

– W.C. Fields

The Plumbers Arms
14 Lower Belgrave Street, Belgravia, SW1W 0LN
02077 304067

Within the upscale streets of Belgravia and amongst elegant townhouses, fine-dining restaurants and luxury shops lies The Plumbers Arms, built in the mid-19th century. Knowing this, it would be safe to assume that this pub would be anything but notorious; however that assumption would be incorrect. It was here in November 1974 that Lady Lucan entered the pub, injured and fearful for her life after discovering that her husband, Lord Lucan had murdered their nanny; Sandra Rivett. This led to Lord Lucan's subsequent disappearance and despite numerous alleged sightings from around the world, Richard John Bingham, 7th Earl of Lucan was never to be seen again.

The Anchor
34 Park Street, Southwark, SE1 9EF
02074 071577

Throughout history, The Anchor, located in Bankside has had many uses over the years besides being a pub. This includes; a chapel, a brothel and ship's chandlers (retail dealer) and records state that the area was used for plague pits in 1603. Dr Samuel Johnson was a close friend of the owners and a regular customer at The Anchor. He wrote many books and poems, the most famous being the dictionary of the English language. A copy of this is now on display inside. It was here at this very pub in 1666 that the famous diarist Samuel Pepys witnessed the Great Fire of London. In his personal diary, he wrote that he took refuge in "a little alehouse on Bankside...and there watched the fire grow".

The Widow's Son

75 Devons Road, Mile End, Bow, E3 3PJ
02030 697426
www.widowsson.co.uk

Sources say that this pub goes back to 1848 when it was a house where a widow lived with her son. Known locally as the "Bun House", this pub carries a story going back 170 years. The Legend of the Widow's Son is that of her only son, who was a sailor that left to go to sea and planned to come back at Easter. In anticipation of his homecoming she saved him a hot cross bun, however he never returned. For the rest of her life, she hung up a bun every Good Friday should he ever return. Since her death, this tradition has continued and every year, a sailor visits the pub to add a new bun to the collection. In 2016, the pub sadly closed and the then owners took the buns with them and Bun Day had to be celebrated elsewhere. But in 2017 when the pub was reopened, the new owners faithfully revived this custom and furthermore, the old buns have since been returned.

LANCASHIRE & GREATER MANCHESTER

LANCASHIRE

GREATER
MANCHESTER

"Q"

"The Rifleman"

"Always remember that I have taken more out of alcohol than
alcohol has taken out of me."

– Winston Churchill

The Old Thirteenth Cheshire Astley
Volunteer Rifleman Corps Inn
9-11 Market Street, Stalybridge, SK15 2AL

Formerly at - 48 Astley Street, Stalybridge, SK15 2EX

Known simply as "The Rifleman" to the locals, this pub is in fact the longest named pub in the UK, as certified by the Guinness Book of Records. The photo above shows the pub at its original location on Astley Street up to 2016 when it closed. After three years of lying dormant, it was re-opened and re-located to Market Street where it lays just two doors away from another record-holding Stalybridge pub.

"Q"
3 Market Street, Stalybridge, SK15 2AL
01613 038893

And from the longest-named pub, we arrive at the shortest-named pub in the country; The "Q" Inn and this also entered the Guinness Book of Records in the same year as "The Rifleman". Who would know that the longest and shortest-named pubs in the United Kingdom would be located not only in the same town, but down the road from one other?

LEICESTERSHIRE

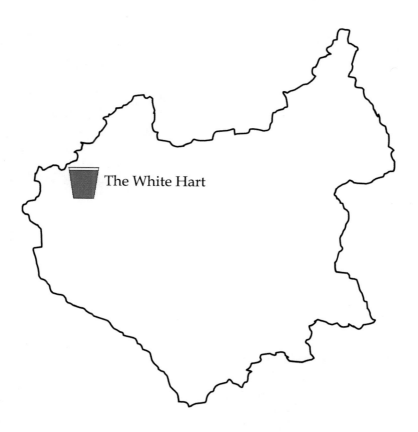

The White Hart

"My grandmother is eighty and still doesn't need glasses. Drinks right out of the bottle."

– Henny Youngman

The White Hart
Market Street, Ashby-de-la-Zouch, LE65 1AP
01530 414531
www.whitehartpubashbydelazouch.co.uk

This pub differs from most because of what used to live in the cellar below; a bear. Years ago when the pub had a reputation for attracting undesirable customers, the landlord would release the bear into the pub should trouble start or if anyone refused to leave.

The place is also claimed to be haunted and it is said that a gallows used to be outside the pub, with numerous sightings being reported of a figure with long hair, floating in mid-air as if they were hanging.

Ashby is built upon a series of tunnels and at one point; two tunnels ran beneath The White Hart which connected to the pub across the road, The Bulls Head and Ashby Castle in the opposite direction.

During renovation work at the pub years previously, a well was found beneath an old cooker and if that wasn't enough, The White Hart used to be frequented often by none other than the famous highwayman Dick Turpin, who regularly visited Ashby on his way down to London.

A stuffed bear can be seen peering through a glass hole in the floor.

LINCOLNSHIRE

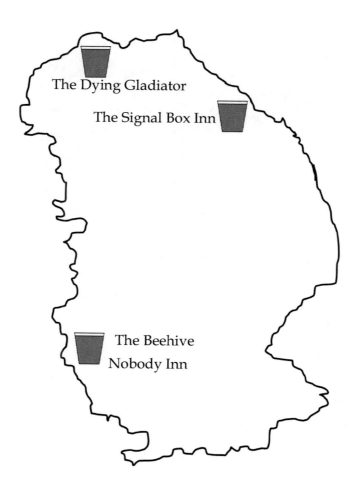

The Dying Gladiator

The Signal Box Inn

The Beehive

Nobody Inn

"Always do sober what you said you'd do drunk. That will teach you to keep your mouth shut."

– Ernest Hemingway

The Beehive
10-11 Castlegate, Grantham, NG31 6SE
01476 404554

Going back to at least 1830, this public house claims to be the only one in the country to have a "living" pub sign. As the name suggests, an actual beehive is nestled in the lime tree outside the pub and has protected status from the local authority. Next to the hive is a poem which reads:

Stop traveller this wonderous sign explore,
And say when thou hast view'd it o'er and o'er,
Now Grantham now two rarities are thine,
A lofty steeple and a living sign.

Nobody Inn
9 North Street, Grantham, NG31 6NU
01476 562206

Sitting on the corner of North and Union Street, this pub has an unusual feature; its name. A popular establishment among the Grantham locals, you can be rest assured that there will always be somebody in.

Image property of The Signal Box Inn

The Signal Box Inn

Cleethorpes Coast Light Railway,
Lakeside Station, Kings Road,
Cleethorpes, DN35 0AG
01472 604657
www.cclr.co.uk/signalboxinn

As the photo suggests, this public house, which was previously a Victorian railway signal box claims to not only be the smallest pub in the country, but on the planet. Despite its small status, the selection of drinks on offer is surprisingly plentiful ~ just don't expect to find a pool table or jukebox inside!

Did you know...

This pub is only 8ft by 8ft squared.

The Dying Gladiator

Bigby Street, Brigg, DN20 8EF
01652 654562

This pub is unique for being the only public house in the country to bear this name and above the front door is an impressive statue of an actual dying gladiator.

NORTHUMBERLAND

The Golden Lion Hotel

"Payday came and with it beer."

– Rudyard Kipling

The Golden Lion Hotel

Market Place, Allendale Town, Hexham, NE47 9BD
01434 683225
www.thegoldenlion.net

This 18th century pub lies in the very heart of Allendale Town and is well worth a visit for many reasons, but for one in particular. Outside here on the 31st December, the Tar Bar'l takes place which is a nothing short of spectacular fire festival that has been a traditional celebration for at least 160 years to welcome in the New Year. The ceremony involves 45 local men known as "guisers" who carry barrels filled with burning hot tar through the town which are then used to ignite the bonfire in the middle of the town square outside the pub.

As the barrels are thrown onto the fire, every man shouts "Be damned to he who throws last." The origin of this tradition is unclear but some believe it began in the Middle Ages, with claims to both Pagan and Christian roots.

NOTTINGHAMSHIRE

Ye Olde Trip to Jerusalem

The Angel Microbrewery

Canalhouse

"You're not drunk if you can lie on the floor without holding on."

– Dean Martin

Canalhouse
48-52 Canal Street, Nottingham, NG1 7EH
01159 555060

Situated next to the main canal in Nottingham, this grade II listed building has an actual canal running through it. The first records of a building here go all the way back to 1796 when it was a warehouse, but after a gunpowder explosion in 1819, it was made into a museum and then finally a bar and restaurant in 2000. The beer garden situated at the rear is at the canal side and to gain access to the bar, one has to cross a footbridge.

Ye Olde Trip To Jerusalem
1 Brewhouse Yard, Nottingham, NG1 6AD
01159 473171

This public house is famous for being England's oldest inn. It is said that King Richard the Lionheart and his fellow crusaders stopped off at the Inn during their journey to Jerusalem in 1189, hence the name.

The pub is reputedly haunted and one of the rooms inside is called the 'Haunted Snug', where a little boy is often seen who was the Master's son; this room being the place he was sent by father when he misbehaved.

Also in the pub is a model of a galleon ship, said to curse and bring death to anyone who cleans it. The model is now in glass, which shows years of built-up dust because of everyone refusing to go near it.

Built partly into the sandstone in which Nottingham Castle sits, there is a museum situated next to the pub allowing visitors to go into the network of caves beneath the building, which were originally used as a brewery.

The Angel Microbrewery
7 Stoney Street, The Lace Market, Nottingham, NG1 1LG
01159 483343
www.angelmicrobrewery.com

This is an interesting pub to say the least and one which dates back to at least the 1600's. Formerly a chapel and a brothel, the Old Angel Inn is located in the historic Lace Market of Nottingham. Below the beer cellar is a cave in the shape of a crucifix. The pub has also been the site of two murders during the 1700's, the victims being a policeman and a prostitute. The prostitute is still said to haunt the building to this day. A few years ago, the pub underwent a major refurbishment and changed its name from the Old Angel Inn to The Angel Microbrewery.

A photo of the pub in 2011.

OXFORDSHIRE

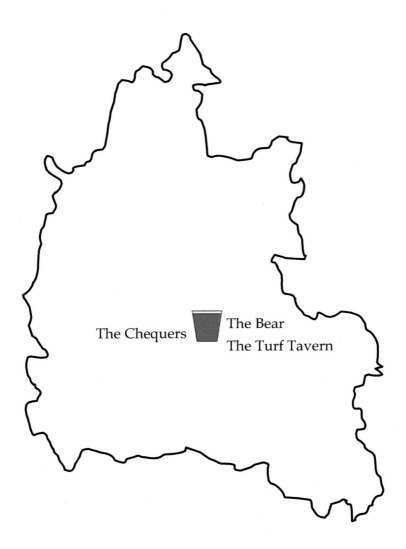

The Chequers   The Bear
                 The Turf Tavern

"I'm not a heavy drinker; I can sometimes go for hours without touching a drop."

– Noel Coward

The Bear Inn
6 Alfred Street, Oxford, OX1 4EH
01865 728164
www.bearoxford.co.uk

This black and white photo shows the very first tie being handed over.

Reputedly the smallest and oldest pub in Oxford, The Bear dates back to 1242 and is famous for its quirky collection of ties dating back to the 1900's. Totaling over 4,000, visitors would hand over their tie in exchange for a pint, to which they are now all on display inside the pub. Tie gentlemen please!

The Chequers
131 High Street, Oxford, OX1 4DH
01865 727463

The earliest record of this pub goes all the way back to 1605, but much of the interior dates back even further to the 1500's. Fast forward two hundred years and The Chequers was the home of various exhibitions such as; conjoined twins and a giant from Hertfordshire. In addition, there were 14 animals on show at the premises, including; a camel from Cairo, a 'sea lioness', an American marsupial, a raccoon and a very large fish, possibly a shark.

IT IS ALLEGED THAT IT WAS HERE AT THE TURF TAVERN THAT BILL CLINTON, WHILE HERE AT OXFORD UNIVERSITY, DURING THE SIXTIES, 'DID NOT INHALE' WHILST SMOKING ILLEGAL SUBSTANCES.
(WHAT HE DOES WITH CIGARS IN HIS OWN TIME IS HIS BUSINESS)

Did you know...

That former Australian Prime Minister Bob Hawke set a Guinness World Record here for drinking a yard glass of beer in 11 seconds.

The Turf Tavern
4-5 Bath Place, Oxford, OX1 3SU
01865 243235

Located off Holywell Street, this well-hidden historic pub lies in the heart of Oxford and used to be the meeting place for illegal gambling. Due to its location just outside the city wall, it managed to avoid the reach of the local governing bodies. A host of famous people have drank here, including; Elizabeth Taylor, Stephen Hawking and Sir Ben Kingsley, but it is probably most famous for being the pub that former US President Bill Clinton frequented during his Oxford University days where he "did not inhale" illegal substances.

"The Turf" was also where the cast and crew of the Harry Potter movies would hang out in between filming.

STAFFORDSHIRE

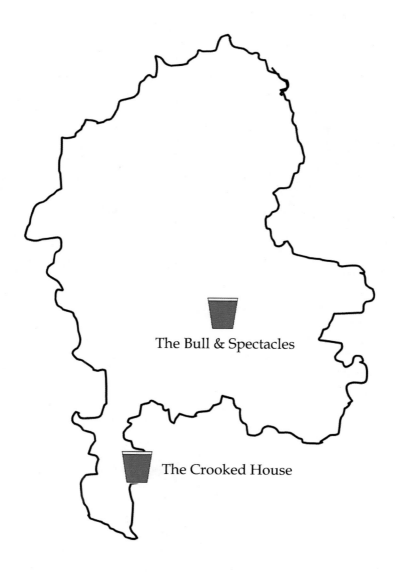

The Bull & Spectacles

The Crooked House

"I would give all of my fame for a pot of ale and safety."

– William Shakespeare

The Crooked House
Coppice Mill, Himley, Dudley, DY3 4DA
01384 238583
www.thecrooked-house.co.uk

Originally built as a farmhouse in 1765, The Crooked House is famous for standing 4ft lower on one side than the other, due to mining subsidence. Previously called 'The Glynne Arms' named after Sir Stephen Glynne on whose estate the pub originally stood and who was brother-in-law to a former Prime Minister, the Right Honourable William Ewart Gladstone. Subsidence occurred during the mid-1800's when mine shafts were dug underneath the site, which then eventually collapsed. Luckily, the pub was saved and support girders and reinforced buttresses were installed, which managed to retain the pub's upright position. When inside, the pub creates an optical illusion where you can see a marble roll uphill and a grandfather clock which looks as if it will fall over at any moment.

The Bull & Spectacles
Uttoxeter Road, Blithbury, Rugeley, WS15 3HY
01889 504201

With parts of the original pub dating back to the 1650's, The Bull & Spectacles has been the subject of much publicity over the years. Originally called The Bulls Head, there is said to be more than one story behind its odd name change. One tale is that one evening; a drunken customer climbed up and placed his glasses on the bull's head, as part of a bet. Another story is that a bull one day walked into the pub and after an altercation, a toilet seat ended up getting stuck in the bull's horns, which could symbolise the 'spectacles'. It is believed to be the only pub in the country with this name, making it even more unique.

TYNE & WEAR

The Marsden Grotto

The Old George

"Alcohol is the anesthesia by which we endure the operation of life."

— George Bernard Shaw

Image property of The Old George

The Old George

Old George Yard, Newcastle-upon-Tyne, NE1 1EZ
01912 603035
www.craft-pubs.co.uk/oldgeorgeinnnewcastle

This pub is not only the oldest pub in Newcastle, but it also has a connection to Royalty. Formerly a coaching inn, this pub is said to have been regularly visited in the 1600's by none other than Charles I, whilst he was serving time in an open prison nearby. Within the pub is the 'Charles I Room' and inside is the chair in which he sat.

The Marsden Grotto
Coast Road, South Shields
NE34 7BS
01914 556060
www.marsdengrotto.com

Also known as "The Grotto", this drinking establishment is famous for being one of few pubs in Europe that is set inside a cave; a 112 ft. cave to be exact. Main access to the pub is via a lift from the cliff above or by navigating a zigzag staircase. Steeped in history, The Marsden Grotto certainly has some interesting stories to tell. In 1782, Jack "Jack the Blaster" Bates a lead miner from Allenheads and his wife Jessie used dynamite from a local quarry to blast a large cave into this cliff, creating themselves a rent-free home. Jack then became involved in smuggling and he and his wife would provide refreshments to smugglers and hidden storage for contraband cargo coming from abroad. "The Grotto" also overlooks Marsden Rock, which is reachable by foot at low tide. In 1803, a flight of stairs was constructed so visitors could walk to the top to take in the amazing views and roughly 100 years later, a choir climbed to the top to give a performance. A poet once said of the rock:

Within the limits of the tidal stream,
A rock arises, bare and tempest riven;
Such a huge ruin might, as a poet's dream,
Be hurled by some proud giant against heaven.
Its base is scooped in many a rugged seam,
Through which the waves are by the wild winds driven,
And hollow arches, crusted o'er with shells,
Are filled or dry, as the sea ebbs or swells.

YORKSHIRE

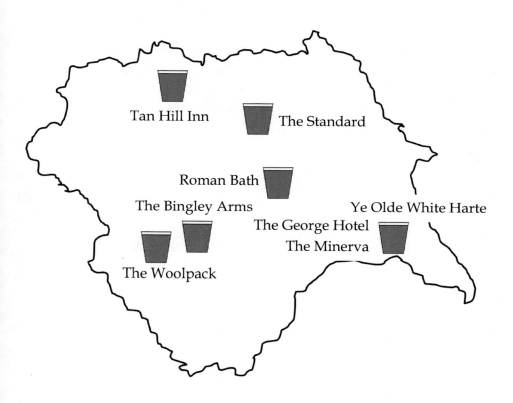

Tan Hill Inn

The Standard

Roman Bath

The Bingley Arms

Ye Olde White Harte

The George Hotel

The Minerva

The Woolpack

"Drink what you want, drink what you're able. If you are drinking with me, you'll be under the table."

– Anonymous

Roman Bath
9 St. Sampson's Square, York, North Yorkshire, YO1 8RN
01904 620455

Here in York or "Eboracum" as the Romans called it, you can visit a pub with an actual Roman bath beneath it. It was discovered in around 1930 and is now a museum that is open to the public. Visitors are able to see what a Roman caldarium looked like. So why not have a drink at the bar and then take a trip back to Roman times.

This photo shows the bathhouse or in Latin; caldarium, located directly beneath the pub.

The Standard
24 High Street, Northallerton, North Yorkshire, DL7 8EE
01609 772719

Image property of The Standard

The name of the pub is in reference to the Battle of the Standard, also known as the Battle of Northallerton, which took place a few miles away in 1138, between the English army, led by William of Aumale and the Scottish army, commanded by King David I.

In the beer garden of this North Yorkshire pub, something quite bizarre sits in it that one will certainly not find anywhere else; an actual aeroplane. Measuring 30ft in length, this Jet Provost aircraft was used as a Royal Air Force trainer jet from 1960 till 1973, based at Linton-on-Ouse airfield near York.

Tan Hill Inn
Tan Hill, Reeth, Richmond, Swaledale
North Yorkshire Dales, DL11 6ED
01833 533007
www.tanhillinn.com

This is the highest pub in the United Kingdom, standing at 1,732 feet above sea level. Built in the 17th century, it was used as a place to sleep for coal pit workers during the 18th century and was aptly named The Kings Pit.

A regular meeting point for walkers and cyclists, not to mention celebrities. It may also be worth noting that people in the past have become stranded at the pub during the winter months. One example is on New Year's Eve in 2009 when 30 people became snowed in for 3 nights, until gritters and snow ploughs were able to reach them.

The Bingley Arms
Church Lane, Bardsey, Leeds
West Yorkshire, LS17 9DR
01937 572462
www.bingleyarms.com

Formerly known as The Priests Inn, this pub has been named in the Guinness Book of Records as officially the oldest public house in Great Britain, dating back as far as 953 AD. Some evidence though suggests that it may even date back to 905 AD. Inside the pub are two priest holes, which are hidden within the chimney. These hideouts provided sanctuary for Catholic priests due to the Dissolution of the Monasteries by King Henry VIII. Beneath the pub was a secret tunnel, which ran between the pub and the local church; All Hallows.

The Woolpack
Main Street, Esholt, West Yorkshire, BD17 7QZ
01274 809495
www.thewoolpackesholt.com

Located in the quaint village of Esholt, the outside of this pub and the village itself was used for the filming of the popular TV soap 'Emmerdale Farm' from 1972 up until 1998. Since then, a replica set of the now renamed 'Emmerdale' has been built on the Harewood Estate in Eccup, near Leeds, although the name of this pub has remained the same. The pub was originally called 'The Commerical Inn' but the name was changed allegedly due to the landlord at the time getting fed up of the TV crew constantly changing the signage when filming exterior shots were needed of the pub.

The Minerva
Nelson Street, Hull, HU1 1XE
01482 210025
www.minerva-hull.co.uk

Establishing itself as a pub in 1829, The Minerva was a regular drinking place for trawlermen who worked up and down the Humber estuary. The pub however is home to the country's smallest pub room or 'snug'.

The George Hotel
Land of Green Ginger, Hull
HU1 2EA
01482 226373

Located on the strangely-named road; Land of Green Ginger, this pub is famous for having the smallest window in the country.

Rumoured to be used during the days when it was a coaching inn, a porter would sit behind the window to watch for guests arriving.

The pub hotel is also supposedly haunted by 'The Grey Lady'.

Ye Olde White Harte

25 Silver Street, Hull, HU1 1JG
01482 326363

Grade II listed, construction began for this building in 1550, but 92 years later, a decision was made at this very pub which some say was the trigger for the English Civil War between King Charles I and Oliver Cromwell. On St George's Day in 1642, King Charles I sent an invitation to dine with the Governor of Hull, Sir John Hotham, as he was

only four miles away from the town. The Governor, retiring to his private room in the pub, now known as 'Ye Plotting Parlour', he sent for Alderman Pelham, the M.P. for the Borough. It was then resolved that the

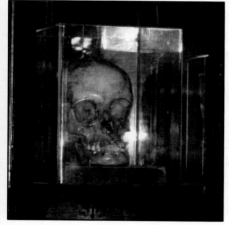

city gates be closed to the King and his followers and entry into the city refused. The King was informed of the decision but nevertheless, the King appeared at the Beverley Gate at around 11 o'clock, but the Governor still refused him entry into Hull through the gates, which were guarded by armed soldiers. After much strong conversation and proclaiming Hotham a traitor, King Charles I withdrew to Beverley.

Around 240 years later in 1881 during restoration work in one of the rooms, human bones including a skull and two swords were found. The skull is believed to be that of a 17 year old girl who appears to have been brutally murdered. The skull can now be seen behind one of the bars in the pub and the two swords are on display above the fireplace in 'Ye Plotting Parlour'.

REST OF THE
UNITED KINGDOM

"Work is the curse of the drinking classes."

– Oscar Wilde

Robinson's Bar
38-40 Great Victoria Street Belfast, BT2 7BA
02890 247447
www.robinsonsbar.co.uk

Established in 1895, this makes it one of Belfast's longest-running drinking establishments. Here, there are five different venues inside, spread over four floors to suit all tastes. One can listen to live Irish music in Fibber Macgees, sample some of the delicious home-cooked food in the Bistro, sing at one of the karaoke nights in BT1 or hustle a few balls in the Pool Loft. Probably the most talked about room though has to be the Saloon, which houses a collection of unique and genuine items that were recovered from the wreckage of the Titanic. On display are things such as; postcards, hand-written letters and the famous Philomena doll. Also on show is a replica lifejacket which was used as a film prop in the 1997 movie, which went on to win 11 Academy Awards.

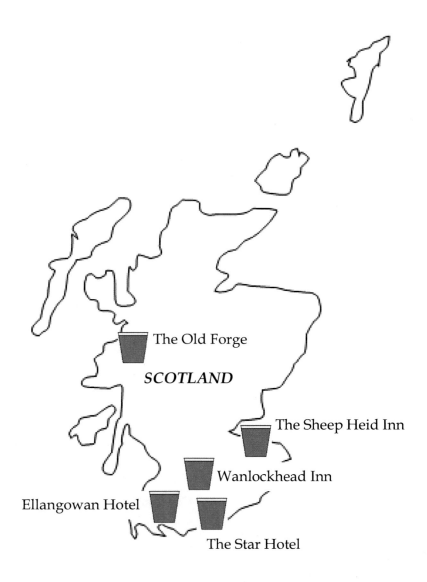

The Old Forge

SCOTLAND

The Sheep Heid Inn

Wanlockhead Inn

Ellangowan Hotel

The Star Hotel

"Beer is proof that God loves us and wants us to be happy."

— Benjamin Franklin

The Old Forge
Inverie, Mallaig, PH41 4PL
01687 462267
www.theoldforge.co.uk

This unique watering hole, which can only be reached by travelling 7 miles on a boat from Mallaig or by walking a total of 18 miles makes it the most remote pub in mainland Britain and they have made it into the Guinness Book of Records to prove it. Starting out as a smiddy's forge (workshop), it became more used as a social club, where it eventually became a pub.

The Famous Star Hotel
44 High Street, Moffat
Dumfries & Galloway, DG10 9EF
01683 220156
www.famousstarhotel.co.uk

Although this is primarily a hotel, it does have two public bars inside. The building dates back to the 1700's and is located on the town's main High Street. As the name suggests, it found fame for being the narrowest hotel on Earth, not just in the United Kingdom, as confirmed by the Guinness Book of Records. The hotel measures only 20 feet in width and 162 feet in length but despite this, it has eight rooms all with en-suite bathrooms, two bars and a restaurant.

The Sheep Heid Inn
43-45 The Causeway, Duddingston
Edinburgh, EH15 3QA
01316 617974
www.thesheepheidedinburgh.co.uk

Image property of Carolyn Jacobs,
The Sheep Heid

Situated in the village of Duddingston next to Holyrood Park, this is reputedly Scotland's oldest surviving public house, as it is said that a pub has stood on this site since 1360. The origin of the name is up for debate, but some say it is named after a snuff box with an embellished ram's head that was given to the Landlord of the pub in 1580 by King James VI of Scotland. The box was kept at the premises until the 19th century where it was sold at auction to the Earl of Rosebery, where it is now kept at Dalmeny House. Another theory comes from the medieval period up until early modern times, where sheep were reared in the royal park behind the pub and were slaughtered before being taken to the Fleshmarket in Edinburgh's Old Town. There being no demand for the heads of the sheep, two dishes were widely remarked upon; sheep heid broth ("powsowdie") and singed sheep heid. In the 18th and 19th century respectively, Bonnie Prince Charlie who was encamped at Duddingston for a month prior to the Battle of Prestonpans will have no doubt drank here with his men leading up to battle, as well as Sir Walter Scott and Robert Louis Stevenson being known regulars. Inside the pub is a skittle alley which dates back to around 1880 and is the country's oldest surviving skittle alley. The last of the old clubs to survive are the Trotters Club who still meet here once a month to play.

This is a photo of the Trotters Club, taken in 1903.

Image property of The Sheep Heid

Wanlockhead Inn
Gardendyke, Wanlockhead
Dumfries & Galloway
ML12 6UZ
01659 74535
www.wanlockheadinn.co.uk

Wanlockhead Inn is Scotland's highest pub, standing 1,531 feet above sea level. Located in Scotland's highest village and a former lead mining community, Wanlockhead. Staying overnight at the Inn involves sleeping in one of their wooden glamping pods to give the feel of camping, but with the comforts of home. Also on site is The Lola Rose Brewery, brewing Beer with Altitude; a range of handcrafted quality Scottish ales.

Ellangowan Hotel
St. John Street, Creetown
Newton Stewart, DG8 7JF
01671 820201
www.ellangowan.co.uk

This pub and hotel lies around halfway between Stranraer and Dumfries and it was here where part of the British cult horror film The Wicker Man was filmed, starring Christopher Lee and Britt Ekland. Released in 1973, the bar area inside doubled as the 'Green Man Inn' public house, where the memorable 'Landlords Daughter' scene was shot. This pub hotel is frequently visited by travellers as part of The Wicker Man location tour.

The Palladium

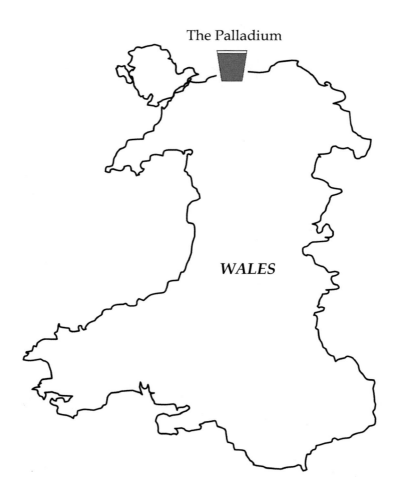

WALES

"Alcohol may be man's worst enemy, but the bible says love your enemy."

— Frank Sinatra

The Palladium

7 Gloddaeth Street, Llandudno, LL30 2DD
01492 863920

Did you know...

The famous actress and singer Dame
Gracie Fields performed here.

Built on the site of Llandudno's market hall, this building first opened as The Palladium Theatre in 1920 where regular variety shows, plays, operas and revues took place.

After WWII, The Palladium served as both a cinema and bingo hall and to accommodate both, the building was divided into two sections.

It eventually closed in 1999 and after comprehensive restoration work, keeping most of its original theatrical features, the grade II listed building was opened in 2001 as a public house by the JD Wetherspoon company.

PUB CHECKLIST ✔

CAMBRIDGESHIRE	
	Charters, Peterborough
	The Regal, Cambridge
	The Eagle, Cambridge
DERBYSHIRE	
	Three Stags' Heads, Wardlow
	Scotsmans Pack, Hathersage
GREATER LONDON & CITY OF LONDON	
	The Plumbers Arms, Belgravia
	The Anchor, Southwark
	The Widow's Son, Bow
LANCASHIRE & GREATER MANCHESTER	
	"The Rifleman", Stalybridge
	Q, Stalybridge
LEICESTERSHIRE	
	The White Hart, Ashby-de-la-Zouch
LINCOLNSHIRE	
	The Beehive, Grantham
	Nobody Inn, Grantham
	The Signal Box Inn, Cleethorpes
	The Dying Gladiator, Brigg
NORTHUMBERLAND	
	The Golden Lion Hotel, Allendale Town
NOTTINGHAMSHIRE	
	Canalhouse, Nottingham
	Ye Olde Trip To Jerusalem, Nottingham
	The Angel Microbrewery, Nottingham

OXFORDSHIRE	
	The Bear, Oxford
	The Chequers, Oxford
	The Turf Tavern, Oxford
STAFFORDSHIRE	
	The Crooked House, Himley
	The Bull & Spectacles, Blithbury
TYNE & WEAR	
	The Old George, Newcastle-upon-Tyne
	The Marsden Grotto, South Shields
YORKSHIRE	
	Roman Bath, York
	The Standard, Northallerton
	Tan Hill Inn, Swaledale
	The Bingley Arms, Bardsey
	The Woolpack, Esholt
	The Minerva, Hull
	The George Hotel, Hull
	Ye Olde White Harte, Hull
NORTHERN IRELAND	
	Robinson's Bar, Belfast
SCOTLAND	
	The Old Forge, Inverie
	The Famous Star Hotel, Moffat
	The Sheep Heid Inn, Duddingston
	Wanlockhead Inn, Wanlockhead
	Ellangowan Hotel, Creetown
WALES	
	The Palladium, Llandudno

FINAL WORD

As this adventure comes to a close, I would like to say a big thank you for reading my book. I hope it has inspired you to go and visit some of these interesting public houses yourself. And as I write this final word, work has already begun on Weird, Wondrous & Historic Pubs of the United Kingdom Part II.

Until next time …

My books can be purchased online in either Paperback or Kindle format from Amazon and are available across their worldwide marketplaces, including; UK, Europe, USA, Canada, Australia and Japan.

I am always interested in hearing from my readers with any feedback, comments or suggestions. If you would like to get in touch, please feel free to drop me a message through the Facebook fan page; *Weird, Wondrous & Historic Pubs of the United Kingdom*.

For regular updates, including; pub photos & information, competitions, comments from industry experts and much more, please join the Facebook fan page.

Made in the USA
Columbia, SC
04 December 2021

50430959R00035